# She Persisted

## HELEN KELLER

—INSPIRED BY—

# She Persisted

by Chelsea Clinton & Alexandra Boiger

# HELEN KELLER

Written by
Courtney Sheinmel

Interior illustrations by
Gillian Flint

PHILOMEL

PHILOMEL BOOKS
An imprint of Penguin Random House LLC, New York

First published in the United States of America by Philomel Books,
an imprint of Penguin Random House LLC, 2021

Visit us online at penguinrandomhouse.com.

Library of Congress Cataloging-in-Publication Data is available.

Printed in the United States of America

HC ISBN 9780593115688
10 9 8 7 6 5 4 3 2 1
PB ISBN 9780593115695
10 9 8 7 6 5 4 3 2 1

WOR

Edited by Jill Santopolo.
Design by Ellice M. Lee.
Text set in LTC Kennerley.

*For*
*Laura Jane Claster*

# She
# Persisted

..................................................................

She Persisted: HARRIET TUBMAN

She Persisted: CLAUDETTE COLVIN

She Persisted: SALLY RIDE

She Persisted: VIRGINIA APGAR

She Persisted: NELLIE BLY

She Persisted: SONIA SOTOMAYOR

She Persisted: FLORENCE GRIFFITH JOYNER

She Persisted: RUBY BRIDGES

She Persisted: CLARA LEMLICH

She Persisted: MARGARET CHASE SMITH

She Persisted: MARIA TALLCHIEF

She Persisted: HELEN KELLER

She Persisted: OPRAH WINFREY

Dear Reader,

As Sally Ride and Marian Wright Edelman both powerfully said, "You can't be what you can't see." When Sally Ride said that, she meant that it was hard to dream of being an astronaut, like she was, or a doctor or an athlete or anything at all if you didn't see someone like you who already had lived that dream. She especially was talking about seeing women in jobs that historically were held by men.

I wrote the first *She Persisted* and the books that came after it because I wanted young girls—and children of all genders—to see women who worked hard to live their dreams. And I wanted all of us to see examples of persistence in the face of different challenges to help inspire us in our own lives.

I'm so thrilled now to partner with a sisterhood of writers to bring longer, more in-depth versions of these stories of women's persistence and achievement to readers. I hope you enjoy these chapter books as much as I do and find them inspiring and empowering.

And remember: If anyone ever tells you no, if anyone ever says your voice isn't important or your dreams are too big, remember these women. They persisted and so should you.

Warmly,

*Chelsea Clinton*

# HELEN KELLER

# TABLE OF CONTENTS

.........................................................

·····························

# Baby Helen

By the time Helen Keller was ten years old, people all around the world knew her story— the little girl from Tuscumbia, Alabama, who was blind and deaf, and who had learned to write and speak. Helen would later use those skills to go to college, write bestselling books, and give speeches around the world. She inspired millions of people to not let their challenges hold them back.

But before all that, Helen was an ordinary baby.

Of course, Helen's parents didn't think she was ordinary. To them, she was precious and extraordinary.

Helen Keller was born on a summer day in 1880. She was a baby who started talking before she was even a year old. Here are some of the first things she said:

*Tea tea tea*

*How d'ye* (an informal way of saying "How do you do?")

*Wah-wah* (Helen's way of saying "water")

Helen was curious and active, too. She loved the sounds of the birds and the colors of the fields and trees on her family's farm. By her first birthday, she'd started to walk. Her parents marveled at all the things she could do. It was a very happy time.

Then something terrible happened. When Helen was just a year and a half old, she became sick. So sick that doctors told her parents she could die. Her body was hot with high fevers. Helen's mother stayed beside her and tried to soothe away all the bad feelings.

Eventually, Helen's fever broke. Her parents were grateful to know that their little girl would live. But they began to notice her life would be different. When Helen's mom moved her hands in front of Helen's face, Helen did not blink. When the bell rang for dinner, Helen didn't turn her head toward the sound like she used to.

Helen couldn't see her mom's hands in front of her face. She couldn't hear the dinner bell. The high fevers had destroyed her hearing and her sight. She was deaf and blind.

Helen's parents called the doctor again. He told them that nothing could be done. Their precious, extraordinary daughter was living in a largely dark and silent world.

Hearing kids learn to speak by listening to other people. How would Helen ever learn to speak if she couldn't hear? How would she learn to read or write if she couldn't see?

Helen herself was too young to realize the seriousness of the situation. Soon, she forgot things had ever been different. She came up with her own signs to communicate without words—head shakes meant *no*, and nods meant *yes*. Pulls meant *come*, and pushes meant *go*. Helen pretended to cut and butter bread when that was what she wanted to eat. If she wanted ice cream, she'd move her hands like she was using the freezer and she'd shiver as if cold.

Helen couldn't see things with her eyes, so she felt with her hands. She ran her fingers over her mother's clothes. She could tell by the style and texture whether her mom was dressed to go out, or whether she'd be staying in. By the time

Helen was five years old, she could fold the laundry and knew how to tell which clothes were her own.

She also figured out what a key was and how to use it. Unfortunately, she once used this skill to lock her mother in the pantry! Her mother was trapped for three hours!

When Helen reached up to her parents' and friends' faces, she could feel their mouths moving as they spoke. She noticed they didn't need signs and signals when they wanted something. Helen tried moving her lips, too. But she didn't have the words to communicate. Even when she used her hand signals, her parents couldn't always tell what she was trying to say.

It was frustrating to have so many thoughts trapped inside her. Sometimes the frustration would boil over and erupt like a volcano. Instead of hot lava, out came strong kicks and loud screams—and she'd keep on kicking and screaming till she was too exhausted to kick and scream anymore.

Life was very hard for young Helen. Would it ever get easier?

....................................

# Changes

Helen's outbursts got worse as she got older. They occurred daily—and sometimes even *hourly.*

She found comfort in her mother's arms, as well as the garden on the family farm. Helen loved the cool feel of the leaves and grass, and the soft scents of the lilies, violets, and especially the roses.

Helen also enjoyed the companionship of her friend Martha, the daughter of the family cook,

and her dog Belle. Martha understood Helen's signs and would usually go along with whatever Helen wanted to do. But Belle was not interested in learning Helen's language—no matter how hard Helen tried to teach her.

When Helen was six years old, another companion entered her life—her younger sister, Mildred.

Mildred did not make a good first impression on her older sister. Helen used to have her mother's lap all to herself. Now Mildred was often there. And that wasn't the only space Mildred had invaded—Helen found the baby sleeping soundly in her beloved doll Nancy's cradle!

Helen was furious. She didn't have words to say how mad she was. So she flipped the cradle over instead.

Her mother caught the baby as she fell. If she hadn't been right there, Mildred could have been seriously hurt.

Another time, Helen spilled water on her apron. She threw it toward the fireplace to dry it.

The apron ignited in flames. They quickly spread to the clothes Helen was wearing. She yelped in fear and pain. Her babysitter heard her cries and threw a blanket over Helen to put out the flames. Luckily, Helen wasn't badly burned.

Helen's parents knew they needed to do something to make their older daughter's world safer and allow her to communicate. But what could they do? There weren't any other kids like Helen in Tuscumbia, Alabama. There weren't any doctors who knew how to treat her.

One day Helen's dad heard about a famous eye doctor named Dr. Chisholm. His office was in Baltimore, Maryland—eight hundred miles away.

Back when Helen Keller was a young girl, you couldn't take an airplane to go to faraway places. Planes hadn't yet been invented! The family

would have to go by train, which would take a long time. The Kellers decided if Dr. Chisholm could help their beloved daughter, the trip would be worth it.

When they got to Baltimore, Dr. Chisholm said he couldn't help Helen after all. But he knew someone who might be able to: Dr. Alexander Graham Bell.

To the world, Alexander Graham Bell was the

inventor of the telephone. But to Helen's parents, he was their next best hope.

Dr. Bell worked in Washington, DC, which meant more train-time for the Kellers. Helen enjoyed the adventure, while her parents continued to fret that there was nothing to be done.

But Dr. Bell had good news for Helen and her parents. He knew about schools and teachers for children who were deaf and blind. He told the Kellers about one school in particular—the Perkins Institute in Boston, Massachusetts. Years earlier at Perkins, a girl named Laura Bridgman who was blind and deaf had been taught to read, write, and communicate.

If the Perkins Institution could help Laura Bridgman, maybe it could help Helen Keller, too.

The Kellers returned home and Helen's dad

contacted the director, Dr. Anagnos, right away. Even though Dr. Bell had already invented the telephone, it would be decades before most people had one in their home. So Helen's dad wrote a letter. He explained that he needed a teacher for his daughter. He mailed the letter, and he and Helen's mom waited anxiously for a reply.

Finally, weeks later, they heard back. A teacher had been found.

Helen's new teacher was named Anne Mansfield Sullivan. She agreed to move in to the Kellers' home to teach Helen.

·····························

# The Most Important
# Teacher

On March 3, 1887, Anne Sullivan arrived in Tuscumbia. Years later, Helen would write that it was the most important day of her life.

Anne had had a hard life. Her eyesight was bad—though she was not totally blind, the way Helen was. She didn't have a family anymore. Maybe her hardships were what made her so determined. She had dreams of teaching Helen to communicate. And buried deep inside of her, Helen had dreams of learning.

But would Anne be able to help her student who was blind, deaf, and unable to speak?

The morning after her arrival, Anne placed a very special doll in Helen's hands. The children at the Perkins Institution had sent it. Laura Bridgman herself had dressed it.

Anne used her fingers to trace letters into Helen's hand:

D·O·L·L

*Doll*

Helen thought it was a fun new game. She copied the letters. She didn't know it, but she had just spelled her first word!

The game continued, with Anne finger-spelling

and Helen copying. Helen spelled lots of new words this way, like:

*Pin*

*Cup*

*Sit*

*Stand*

Helen was a fast learner. But there was a lot she needed to be taught, and things were still hard. She didn't know how to communicate all that she wanted to say. In those moments, she had a terrible temper. It wasn't her fault. But it made her difficult to be around.

Anne decided Helen needed to learn some new habits. To do that, she needed a change of scene. Together, Anne and Helen moved out of the main house and into a small cottage. For two weeks, it was just teacher and student. Anne was strict with Helen, and Helen did not like it one bit. She pinched and kicked her teacher. She even knocked out one of her teeth!

Other teachers may have left. But Anne did not give up! She taught Helen to sit at the table for meals, to eat with a knife and fork, to dress herself, and to spell words—words, words, and more words!

Helen started to understand that the words she was learning were names for things. But it was hard. How do you teach someone who can't hear and can't see that the water they drink is different from the mug they drink from? How do you explain that water can be in a mug, or come from a well, or flow through a river or an ocean?

Anne took Helen outside. She placed one of

Helen's hands under the well's spout and spelled into her other palm: W-A-T-E-R.

She spelled it over and over, faster and faster.

*Wah-wah* had been one of little Helen's first words, before she got sick. For years, that word had been hiding in the back of her brain. Now,

as the cool stream gushed over Helen's hand, she felt the spark of that memory. She knew what water was.

The world was opening up, and Helen was eager to learn more. She touched every object she could get her hands on. Anne taught her the words for all of them. Learning made Helen more confident and happier. She stopped having so many tantrums.

Anne's next challenge was to teach Helen the words for abstract ideas. That means words that don't refer to specific objects. They're harder for all kids to learn.

Anne decided to start with the word *love*. She tapped Helen's chest, pointing to her heart. Helen did not understand.

A couple days later, Helen was having trouble

stringing beads together. Anne spelled *T·H·I·N·K* on her forehead.

*Think.*

It was a word for an abstract idea, just like the word *love*. In a flash, Helen understood that *think* was the word for the process going on in her head.

The next time Anne tried to explain *love*, Helen understood. It was not an object. She could not touch it. But she could, as she later wrote, "feel the sweetness that it pours into everything."

Helen loved to learn. She loved the world. And she loved her teacher.

. . . . . . . . . . . . . . . . . . . . . . . . . . . . . . .

## *Life Lessons*

Helen no longer needed to shake or nod her head. She didn't need to push and pull. She didn't need to mime what she wanted to eat. By using her finger-spelling, she could talk!

Anne taught Helen more and more. They both loved the outdoors. Anne came up with creative ways to use nature in their lessons. Using mud, pebbles, and water, they made their own dams, islands, and lakes. Anne molded clay into maps. Helen felt the mini mountain ridges and valleys.

Next up was teaching Helen to read. It would be another challenge, since Helen couldn't see the words on the page.

Anne gave Helen slips of cardboard that had raised letters of the alphabet printed on them. Helen didn't have to *see* them. She could *feel* them. Later, Anne gave Helen a book with the words written in those same raised letters. Helen ran her fingertips along the words, searching for the ones she recognized.

Reading quickly became one of Helen's favorite activities. Later, Helen explained: "More than any other time, when I hold a beloved book in my hand my limitations fall from me, my spirit is free."

Helen read to herself, to her baby sister,

Mildred, and to Belle the dog, all by spelling the sentences out with her fingers. Mildred was too little to understand what Helen was doing, and Belle didn't always stick around for story time— but that didn't stop Helen!

Anne also taught Helen to read braille. Braille is a special written language for people who are blind—each letter is represented by a series of raised dots, which can be read by feeling them. Anne wrote letters all about Helen's incredible progress to Dr. Anagnos, the director of the Perkins Institution, up in Boston.

In May of 1888, Anne took Helen to meet everyone at Perkins. Helen felt right at home. She played with other children who were blind and who knew how to communicate by spelling into each other's hands, just like she did.

From then on, Helen spent almost every winter in Boston. One day Helen heard about a young boy named Tommy who was deaf and blind, just like she was. Tommy's family couldn't afford to pay for Tommy's education on their own. Helen thought every kid who needed it should be able to attend Perkins, so she began to save her pennies. She asked her friends for contributions, too. When her dog died, people offered to help buy her another dog. But Helen told them no; instead she wanted the money to go toward Tommy's school fund. The fund grew fast, and little Tommy was admitted to Perkins.

Helen knew that outside of Perkins, most other people used another method of communication— they spoke out loud. She was determined to do it herself. Anne didn't know how to teach Helen to speak. Luckily, Anne found another teacher who did. Her name was Sarah Fuller. She put Helen's hands over her face. Helen could feel how Sarah's tongue and lips moved when she spoke. By the end of the first lesson, Helen could say several letters.

But when Helen tried to speak, it was hard for anyone to understand what she was saying. She practiced day and night. Whenever she felt discouraged, she would think about being able to speak to her family—especially to her younger sister, Mildred. Those thoughts inspired her to work even harder. "I am not dumb now," Helen said out loud to herself. In those days, the word *dumb* was used to describe people who could not speak out loud. Helen meant that she now could.

Helen was focused on this goal. But perhaps what she didn't realize was it would also have been okay if she *hadn't* learned to speak. The ability to speak didn't make Helen who she was; it was everything she was in her mind and her heart that mattered.

Given Helen's love of words, it is no surprise she started writing her own stories. Dr. Anagnos's birthday was coming up. Helen wrote him a story called "The Frost King." Everyone

loved it, especially Dr. Anagnos. He had it pub-lished in the Perkins alumni magazine.

Then someone discovered that Helen's story was nearly exactly the same as another writer's story, "The Frost Fairies." They said she had copied it. Helen didn't remember ever reading the other story—but she knew she must have. She had not done it on purpose and she was devastated.

Dr. Anagnos was upset, too. He felt Helen and Anne had purposely deceived him. They went home to Alabama. It was such a terrible experience that Helen never spent the winter at the Perkins Institution ever again.

...............................

## CHAPTER 5

## *Dream It, Do It*

Helen was scared to write anything else for a long time. What if she accidentally copied someone else's work again?

But Anne knew that writing was good for Helen. She encouraged Helen to trust herself. Finally, Helen wrote a piece about her life for a publication called *Youth's Companion*. She was twelve years old.

Helen also wanted to continue her education.

She'd worked so hard to learn to speak English. Now she was interested in other languages, like French and Latin. Even though she was not in school, she studied a lot. She also practiced her speaking skills. She read out loud to Anne and recited her favorite passages from memory.

When she was fourteen years old, Helen began attending the Wright-Humason School for the Deaf in New York City, where she studied French, German, math, and geography. In her free time, she explored the city, visiting Central Park and the Statue of Liberty, among other places. Even though she couldn't see or hear, her other senses worked and she could feel what was happening. Her visits to lower-income neighborhoods left an especially lasting impression. Later in her life, Helen would do all she could to help those less fortunate than she was, those with fewer resources or less money than her family had.

While in New York, Helen also worked on her lipreading. It was very hard for Helen to read lips. She had to put her hands on the speaker's mouth to feel the words. She continued practicing her speech, too. She had a dream: to speak as clearly as hearing people spoke.

Helen tried her best. But that dream did not ever come true. Her speech would always sound different. Her handwriting looked different from other people's, too. The letters were boxier, but they were still easy to read.

Even if Helen didn't achieve every goal she set, her accomplishments were remarkable. Soon, she set a new goal for herself: she wanted to go to college.

Back when Helen was a teenager, most girls didn't think about going to college. And they *couldn't* go to the college Helen wanted to go to— Harvard. Harvard only let in male students.

Helen decided to apply to Harvard's sister school, Radcliffe.

Radcliffe was one of the best schools in the country. It was not an easy school to get into. No one who was deaf and blind ever had. But Helen was determined to be the first. She left New York to go to the Cambridge School for Young Ladies, a special school that prepared students for Radcliffe.

Helen had never before studied alongside students who could see and hear. She worked very hard—and so did Anne. Most of Helen's textbooks were unavailable in braille, so Anne spelled the words into Helen's hands. Later, Helen

studied algebra, geometry, Greek, and Latin with a private tutor. Anne continued to finger-spell all the lessons.

But when it came time to take the tests to get in, the people at Radcliffe said that Anne was not allowed into the testing room to spell out the questions. Instead the college hired someone named Mr. Vining to come in and copy the papers in braille. It was much harder for Helen this way—especially when it came to math, her least favorite subject. Mr. Vining used a different braille system than the one Helen knew. When the tests were finally over, she was sure that she had failed.

But Helen met her goal again! Her test scores were high enough to get into Radcliffe!

Of course, there was more hard work once she started college. Much more. Anne sat right next

to Helen in every class. She spelled the professors'
words and the textbook reading assignments into
Helen's hands. It all took a very long time—longer
than it took any of the other students, who could
hear the professors and read the books on their
own. At the end of each day, Helen didn't have
any extra time left over to relax, play, or daydream.

Helen had always been a hardworking
student. But Radcliffe was
even harder than she had
expected. It was lone-
lier, too. Helen did not
give up. She earned
her bachelor of arts
degree with honors—
that means her grades
were higher than most of

the other people in her classes. She was the first person who was blind and deaf to graduate from college. She would not be the last.

Helen started writing her autobiography while she was still in college. *The Story of My Life* was published when she was only twenty-two years old. It was the story of her life—*so far.* Helen still had a lot of living to do!

............................

# Helen's Legacy

Helen Keller had learned to read and write, even though she lived during a time when there weren't many resources for people who were blind and deaf, or had other disabilities. She'd learned to speak. She'd gone to college, and graduated with honors. She'd written a book, which was translated into fifty languages and read by people all around the world. What more would she accomplish? A lot more.

After *The Story of My Life*, Helen wrote thirteen other books, along with countless articles and speeches. She traveled to thirty-nine countries. Lots of famous people wanted to meet her, including world leaders like Winston Churchill, who was the prime minister of England; Golda Meir, who would later become the prime minister of Israel; and every president of the United States from Grover Cleveland to John F. Kennedy.

Helen became very famous herself. She used her fame to improve the lives of others. She was an advocate for people with disabilities. Being an advocate means supporting someone or something. And that's what she did!

In 1915, Helen co-founded the American Foundation for Overseas Blind, which helped soldiers who were blinded in World War I. It's now known as Helen Keller International, and it works on behalf of people who are blind, don't have enough to eat, or are in poor health.

Helen also fought for other causes, like workers' rights and women's suffrage—which is the right for women to vote in political elections. Women didn't win that right in the United States till 1920! That same year, Helen helped start an organization called the American Civil Liberties

Union, or ACLU for short. To this day, the ACLU works to protect people who are being discriminated against.

Throughout her life, Helen had the support of people who understood her needs—her family, her friends, and especially her teacher, Anne Sullivan.

Anne stayed by her student's side for nearly fifty years. By that point, they were no longer just student and teacher; they were each other's family. After Anne's death in 1936, a woman named Polly Thomson took over helping Helen. Helen continued to travel, give speeches, raise awareness of causes that were important to her, and make a difference in other people's lives. She became one of the most admired women of the twentieth century.

In 1959, there was a Broadway show about Helen's life and her work with Anne called *The Miracle Worker*. Three years later, it was turned into an Academy Award–winning movie.

By then, Helen had had a stroke. She mostly stayed in her home in Westport, Connecticut. Just a few weeks before her eighty-eighth birthday, she died in her sleep.

Helen Keller once said, "The true test of character is to face hard conditions with the determination to make them better." That is her legacy. She made the world better with her determination—for herself, and for other people who faced hard conditions, too. The organizations she helped start continue to do important work. Schools founded in Helen's name educate and empower students to this day. The example of her life changed the way people think about those who are blind and deaf.

Helen Keller accomplished things that no one could have imagined back when she was a little girl who could not speak or read. But Helen persisted. Her life is a lesson for us all to work hard to achieve our dreams, no matter the obstacles, and to help other people whenever and wherever we can along the way.

# HOW YOU CAN PERSIST

*by Courtney Sheinmel*

If you would like to help carry on Helen Keller's legacy, here are some things you can do:

1. If you know someone with a disability or any kind of difficulty, ask them what you can do to help.

2. Stop other people from making fun

of those those who are disabled, or different in any way.

3. Find out if you can help raise a puppy who can later be trained as a therapy pet, like a seeing-eye dog.

4. Read to people who cannot read to themselves—for example, young children, or people who are blind and can't read braille books.

5. Organize a bake sale, a car wash, a walk-a-thon, or any other kind of fundraiser to raise money for Helen Keller International or the ACLU.

6. Read a book about Helen's very special teacher, Anne Sullivan.

7. Tell your friends the story of Helen Keller. Tell them how she persisted in learning to read and write and speak. Tell them how she found her voice and used it to help others.

# Acknowledgments

······································

My deepest thanks—

To Chelsea Clinton, for creating the Persisterhood and for trusting me with Helen Keller's story; to Alexandra Boiger for the magnificent cover; and to Gillian Flint for the beautiful illustrations in between the covers.

To the remarkable Helen Keller, who has been an inspiration to me ever since I did my third-grade biography report about her in 1986; and to a few people close to Ms. Keller who enriched her life: her devoted and unrelenting teacher, Anne Sullivan, and her loving and brave parents, Kate and Arthur Keller.

To Jill Santopolo Claster, for being an incredible editor and an even better friend; to Talia Benamy, for her invaluable notes; to Krista Ahlberg and Shara Hardeson, for their careful readings of the manuscript; to Ellice Lee, Shanta Newlin, and the team at Philomel Books; and to my agent, Laura Dail, for more things than I have room to list here.

To my partner, Zac Cherry, for his unwavering love and support, and for supplying all the M&M's; to the good people of Sesame Street who created programming to keep my son, Archer, occupied while I wrote; and to my sweet Archer Wolf Maxwell—not for anything in particular, Archie; just for being you and for being mine.

Finally and especially—to the legacy of magnificent women throughout history whose persistence simultaneously awes and emboldens me. Special shout-out to my mother, Elaine Sheinmel, who is ever the model of showing up, being kind, trying hard, making the best of it, and persisting.

# ❦ References ❧

## BOOKS

Herrmann, Dorothy. *Helen Keller: A Life.*
University of Chicago Press, 1999.

Keller, Helen. *The Story of my Life.* New York:
The Modern Library, 2004. (Originally
published in 1903.)

Keller, Helen. *The World I Live In*. New York:
The New York Review of Books, 2003.
(Originally published in 1908.)

## ONLINE RESOURCES

Gordon, Jamie. "Helen Keller, advocate and
traveler." Perkins School for the Blind.
August 18, 2015. https://www.perkins.org
/stories/helen-keller-advocate-and-traveler.

"Helen Keller." Perkins School for the Blind.
https://www.perkins.org/history/people
/helen-keller.

"Helen Keller Biography." American Foundation
for the Blind. https://www.afb.org/about-afb
/history/helen-kellerbiography-and-chronology
/biography#family.

"Helen Keller Biography." Biography.
February 27, 2020. https://www.biography
.com/activist/helen-keller.

Helen Keller Intl. https://www.hki.org.

"Helen Keller Quotations." American Foundation
for the Blind. https://www.afb.org/about-afb
/history/helen-keller/helen-keller-quotes.

*The Miracle Worker* (1962). IMDb. https://www
.imdb.com/title/tt0056241.

*The Miracle Worker* (1959). Internet Broadway
Database. https://www.ibdb.com
/broadway-production/the-miracle-worker-2759.

COURTNEY SHEINMEL is a chocolate-lover, mac 'n' cheese expert, mom to Archer, and the author of nearly thirty books for kids and teens, including several series for young readers—Stella Batts, My Pet Slime, Magic on the Map (co-written with Bianca Turetsky), and Agnes & Clarabelle (co-written with Adele Griffin). She received a National Scholastic Outstanding Educator Award for her work as a writing instructor at the non-profit Writopia Lab.

Photo credit: Jennifer E. Daly

You can visit Courtney Sheinmel online at
courtneysheinmel.com
or follow her on Twitter
@courtneywrites

GILLIAN FLINT has worked as a professional illustrator since earning an animation and illustration degree in 2003. Her work has since been published in the UK, USA and Australia. In her spare time, Gillian enjoys reading, spending time with her family and puttering about in the garden on sunny days. She lives in the northwest of England.

You can visit Gillian Flint online at
gillianflint.com
or follow her on Twitter
@GillianFlint
and on Instagram
@gillianflint_illustration

CHELSEA CLINTON is the author of the #1 *New York Times* bestseller *She Persisted: 13 American Women Who Changed the World*; *She Persisted Around the World: 13 Women Who Changed History*; *She Persisted in Sports: American Olympians Who Changed the Game*; *Don't Let Them Disappear: 12 Endangered Species Across the Globe*; *It's Your World: Get Informed, Get Inspired & Get Going!*; *Start Now!: You Can Make a Difference*; with Hillary Clinton, *Grandma's Gardens* and *Gutsy Women*; and, with Devi Sridhar, *Governing Global Health: Who Runs the World and Why?* She is also the Vice Chair of the Clinton Foundation, where she works on many initiatives, including those that help empower the next generation of leaders. She lives in New York City with her husband, Marc, their children and their dog, Soren.

*Courtesy of the author*

You can follow Chelsea Clinton on Twitter
@ChelseaClinton
or on Facebook at
facebook.com/chelseaclinton

ALEXANDRA BOIGER has illustrated nearly twenty picture books, including the She Persisted books by Chelsea Clinton; the popular Tallulah series by Marilyn Singer; and the Max and Marla books, which she also wrote. Originally from Munich, Germany, she now lives outside of San Francisco, California, with her husband, Andrea, daughter, Vanessa, and two cats, Luiso and Winter.

Photo credit: *Vanessa Blasich*

You can visit Alexandra Boiger online at
alexandraboiger.com
or follow her on Instagram
@alexandra_boiger

# Don't miss the rest of the books in the

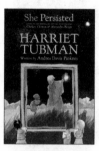

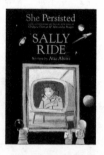

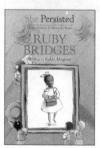

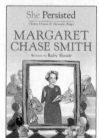

# She Persisted series!

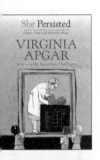

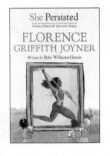

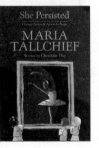

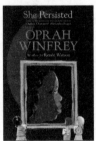